CW00631373

Pie and Papier-Mâché

Daniel Cockrill

trinovantes

First published in 2007 by Trinovantes

www.trinovantes.co.uk

ISBN 978-0-9557227-0-7

1 3 5 7 9 10 8 6 4 2

A CIP catalogue record for this book is available from the British Library.

Jacket design by Kenosha
Illustration by Martin Galton

Printed and bound in Great Britain by TJ International, Padstow

Contents

for the lure in failure and the magic in Gina

The My Poems

My Geography Teacher

Mr Jenkins
did not like us loitering
but he did like the word undulating

once I thought about him
undulating with his wife
it was not a nice thought

he preferred the geography
of the land
more than the geography
of the body

his first name was Aubrey
he always wore corduroy
he was a welsh boy-o.

My Toaster

i don't like to boast
but i've got a great toaster
it makes great toast
in fact i think it's the best thing since slice bread

My Bed

lately
my bed has been
like Clapham Junction
but luckily
there hasn't been
a head on collision.

there's been no delays
i've come on time
and sometimes early
which also leaves
the customer disgruntled.

there's no pleasing
some people.

My Ex-Girlfriend

Janette
should go visit a vet
coz i think she's a dog

My Shower

my shower
has great power

Boys

Alan

Alan
whose wife is Belgian
or was it German
is a coach driver
well so he seems to think
he'll drive you round the bend
he'll drive you to the brink
when he should be driving you
to Amsterdam.

he'll send you on the scenic route
and we'll send him to Coventry
or if we're lucky
to prison.

Alan drives long distance
and when he's away
his wife drives the milkman wild
he delivers two pints of full cream
past-her-eyes.

George

George lost his temper with me
for no apparent reason.
i told him to keep his hair on.
George is bald.

Stan The Man

he is the most
beautiful
man in the
world.

when he laughs
i am happy
for him
when he sleeps
i am happy
for him
when he hugs
his mum and dad
i am happy
for them.

a stranger
may not see that
he is the most
beautiful
man in the world.

to us
the world is
confusing
but to him
it is like
clouds
on a clear day
or blue sky
when it should be
grey.

his mum sits
on the sofa
crying
she is tired
because her son is
alone
not from lack of
love
but because his
burden
is to be
alone.

to be the most
beautiful
man in the
world
you must be
alone.

his brother Victor
loves him
his brother cares
for him
when he cries
Victor says
mum
dad
Stanley is
crying
he cares for his
brother
he loves him
dearly.

to suffer this
a punishment
the rewards must be
great
a reward
unseen.

the boy
on his dads back
is the most
beautiful
boy in the
world.

sometimes you feel
that you want
to get
hold of him
to squeeze him
to squeeze him
so tight
that you might
squeeze out
of him his condition

but this may also
squeeze out his
beauty

for he is the most
beautiful
man in the world.

Girls

Nina's Poem

i have seen 'er
her name is Nina
i want to hold her
hug her
and squeeze her
but i think that would displease her
                              boyfriend

Paula's Poem

i want all a'
Paula
i want to pull 'er

Poonam's Poem

i knew a girl called Poonam
her friends called her Poo for short
which is a bit of a shitty nickname if you ask me

A Poem About A Girl From Helsinki

i'd like to get kinky
with the girl from Helsinki

when i'm cheeky
do you go all leaky?

when i'm cocky
do you want to be my jockey?

are you a bit sticky?
do you fancy a quickie?

can i be sneaky
and take a quick peaky
of your leaky
streaky
creeky?

shall we keep it low key
or shall we do the Hokey Cokey?

okey dokey
in out
in out
shake it all about

now i'm feeling lucky
can i make you mucky?
but i'll clean you up
as if i was a clean up tissue
from Kentucky... Fried Chicken

cos
i'd like to get kinky
with the girl from Helsinki.

Carly's Poem

Angela and Carly strut their stuff
boys wanting to stroke their hairy...hair
but these two girls don't seem to care
sharing secrets
their sexuality warming boys like heaters
these two maniac chocolate eaters
the chocoholics
living for cheap feels
                frills
                and frolics
just looking for a stalagmite
to suck the lime off in the night
the bigger the better
the warmer the wetter
i want to let her and her
do their dirty deeds
so that i can sow my seeds
well we all have needs
                     don't we...

Birth Mark On The Bum

for what it's worth
it's been there since birth
smudged on Angela's wide

                          backside

it's part of her identity
a feature i would like to see
and so would Tony

                 Smith

so show us your bum and clear up this myth
just a quick peek
of your bum cheek
that's all it would take to make my week.

A Poem About My Neighbour

Nina's my neighbour
i lent her my Hoover
cos i want to suck up to her
and for her to be my loover.

Rain And PMT Haiku

i think all in all
girls are unpredictable
unlike the weather.

Family

My Old Man

my old man said
i'd never amount to anything
guess what
he was right
wise old fool

For Those Who Knew Their Father

I remember the time when I thought my father was all knowing, he had all the answers to all the questions and all the tricks to fix things. I can't remember finding out when all that changed. I think it's hard being better educated than your father (for both parties) and that's why I won't be sending my kids to university. This is for my father.

My father is

a beer on Sunday

a mop and a bucket

a dead son

a caged bird

a crib board

a cowboy boot

a Willie Nelson record

a 5am alarm clock

a Reader's Digest magazine

a chamois leather

a garage full of junk

a loft full of junk

a Bobby Moore poster

a boxed electric train set

a saddle on the dashboard

a ladder on the roof rack

a fountain pen

a small change moneybag

a lone drinker

a spaghetti western

a stetson

a red and grey beard

a bushy eyebrow

a taxi to the station

a ten pound note

a twenty pound note

a snooze on the sofa

a tabloid paper

an unfinished crossword.

My Gramp's Nut

i watched as he peeled that chestnut
his hands frail
not as good as they used to be
i envied his patience
leaning
chipping off the outer shell
concentrating
it took my grandad at least four minutes
to peel that nut
to reveal that nut
i smiled
pleased that he had a whole chestnut
to eat all by himself
slowly
he lifted his four minute effort
towards his mouth
his hands frail
not as good as they used to be
you could almost taste
that crisp sweet crunch
then it happened
he dropped the nut
and before anyone could say
"watch the dog"
the nut vanished into the dog's stomach
that was my gramp's nut.

Blind Grandad

he was a library full of gossip
he'd wade through tabloid paper
to gather facts together
he'd sip on home brewed bitter
his wife would cook the dinner
gammon steak and mashed potato
uprooted from his garden
in the winter.

Gina's Gravy

gives a mediocre roast
something to boast about

what the world needs
is Gina's gravy

to end all poverty
to end all wars

get off your navy boat
drink from Gina's gravy boat.

consume on Sundays
tell me why I don't like Mondays?

cos I've got no gravy

if you want to be a winner
put some gravy on your dinner

forget the whale
forget the seal
save the gravy
on your meal

her gravy
my favourite liquor
helps me dinner
go down much quicker

lap it up with your finger

grieve for the naive
who believe in and crave
the gravy
granule
pave the way
say No
to Bisto

she'll take her gravy
to the grave
the gift she gave
Gina's gravy.

Mama, Don't Let Your Babies Grow Up

Mama
don't let your babies grow up to be
choirboys

Love

Love Poem

je t'aime
iced gem.

The Cost Of Loving

it doesn't cum cheap
to penetrate deep

Sharing

we share a bed
so I can't see why
we shouldn't share
a sock drawer

More Sharing

How long did
you share
your shower?

We shared
our shour
for an hour.

I Love You More

i love you more
than poets love rhyme
i love you more
than Einstein loved time
i love you more
than coppers love crime
i love you more

i love you more
than china loves tea
i love you more
than honey loves bee
i love you more
than a narcissist loves me
i love you more

i love you more
than Midas loved gold
i love you more
than ice cubes love cold
i love you more
than origami loves to fold... paper
i love you more

i love you more
than dampness loves mould
i love you more
than an archaeologist loves old
i love you more
than an auctioneer loves to say sold
to the man at the front with the moustache
i love you more

i need you more
than the night sky needs the stars
i need you more
than wonder needed bras
i need you more
than green men need Mars... bars
i need you more

i love you more
than the length of a piece of string
i love you more
than A. Bell loved to ring
i love you more
than Gene Kelly loves to sing
in the rain
what a glorious feeling
i'm happy again
i love you more

Elegies

Pebble

to build castles in sand
only to be knocked down by the tide
wall of grain by wall of grain.

to miss my friend as much
as he misses the sun
in the artic winter.

to splinter my thoughts with sorrow;

to not know the place
or the back of my hand
to miss my friend
the fading castle
the sand.

Life Without You

blossom bloom
blossom moss
blossom fall
blossom loss
blossom less
that is life without you
I guess.

Elegy 1

today i miss my brother
because my dad cried
today i wish for my brother
because my mum is so unhappy
i'm afraid
God got it wrong.

Elegy 2

sweet smoke
soak you in flame
drown me in whiskey

you drank a lot of whiskey
when Ashoka died
did it work
"yes" you replied
but now i know
you lied.

Poem

tear my paper heart
confetti
or just ripped up paper

fold my paper heart
origami
and make a fragile china cup

drop my fragile heart
and watch it break

take the pieces and make
a pattern so pretty
and emptied of pain

drop my fragile heart
and watch it break
drop my fragile heart

Poem

when my chest grows tight
and i reach the point
when i feel i cannot breathe
i stop
and hold my breath
for as long as is humanly possible.

hoping i might drown
hoping i might come up gasping
hoping i might leave
the heavy weight of pain
shipwrecked at the bottom.

Death

D. I. Why?

why did Di die
the day i did my D.I.Y?
i don't know why Di died
the day i did my D.I.Y
why?
i don't know why, do i, Di.

In Manchester
the girls do not wear
many clothes.
And what they do wear
is tight
and revealing.

If I have a terminal illness
I will go to Manchester.

I will not be cured of my illness
but I will die happily aroused.

sped across rail
in Kent
towards Charing Cross
i'm cross
she is heaven sent
in return she has lent them her father
maybe she gets him back
on the return journey.

Politics

Message To The President

George W. Bush
       Shush!!!

Bus Inspector

Hans Blix
was on the two, one, four

but he couldn't prevent a war.

Terrorism

Apparently
These are dangerous times
But danger for me
Is writing poetry
Under falling scaffolding

I live in terror.

Picking Holes In The State Of Things

today
i'm not making my usual way down the pub
why?
cos i'm going to Job Club

if you aint got a job – join the club
if you aint got a life – join the club
if you can't compete
and you need to get back on your feet
join the Job Club

now
Janet is the leader of Job Club
and Janet's a real Janet
next time you give a lesson
                    plan it
Janet says "you can be anything you want to be
you can practice your C.V.
you get a free cup of tea
but if you want a refill
you have to pay 10p"
                    at the Job Club.

in the group is Dave
who raves on about how good he is
he is the biz
well so he says
he aint got a job
but he's got a big gob

and poor eyesight
he can't even see beyond the lenses in his glasses
and he's got a bad haircut too
but he believes he's the best
and the rest of 'em who've got jobs
don't deserve 'em
even guide dogs don't deserve 'em
Dave says "i've got loads of qualifications me"
it's not that you're not qualified Dave
it's just that you're a pain in the neck mate.

Tracey enjoys Job Club
she joined the same day as me
and bless her
she wants to be a hairdresser

she says her husband only makes £240 a week
so she is seeking work
to perk up his wages
cos it's been ages since they went out together
and left the kids at home
                              little bastards.

what Tracey wants is £3.80 an hour
Dave he wants 4
Gordon is a manager
and he wants so much more
like 16 grand
cash in hand
a plot of land

to build a house
and a company car
    far too greedy.

"well Dan" says Janet
"what do you do?"
"what... me!
well, i get up at one to eat a slice of toast
but that'll be the most i do
cos i go a bed again at two."
"but Dan" says Janet
"what do you think, how do you feel
 about Job Club?"
Dan pauses and takes a deep breath
"honestly, truthfully i admit,
 i didn't learn jack shit"
    at Job Club.

so when things are a mess
and you're jobless
please remember that at Job Club
at least you do get a free cup of coffee
but you couldn't work for toffee.

Religion

Easter

What's so good about Friday?
And you, get back in your cave,
you're meant to be dead.

Jesus And Me

i taught Jesus
a thing or two

i stuck a leper's arm on
with super glue

i turned water into wine
i drank so much
in one day
my wee came out
as Beaujolais

what a shocker
i can piss Rioja

i fed the five thousand
by cutting a loaf
into very small pieces
usually referred to as crumbs

i walked on water
with the help of a speed boat

Jesus went into the desert
for forty days
which isn't a miracle
but it's pretty fucking good

i on the other hand
went into the kitchen
for forty days
and ate nothing
but dessert

i came out looking like
Big Daddy chanting

"Easy, Easy...Poetry!"

i don't claim to be
the Number 1 Jew
but i did teach Jesus
a thing or two.

Was Jesus French?

je suis
Jesus

It's Not Just The Ref Who Is Blind

i dreamt i was Jesus
a professional footballer
playing football for Bethlehem City
against Manchester United

in full flight
i skipped past three defenders
one
two
past the last
       blasting down the wing
              the crowd sing
     "Jesus, Jesus, Jesus is King"

with that in mind
i tried to put in a good cross
but instead i was nailed to a bad one

"two nail, two nail"

and God said
"on me head son."

Travel

In Flight Entertainment

when i look up to the sky
and i see an aeroplane

i don't think of holidays
and trips to Spain

i don't think of transport
a bus or train

i don't think of famous passengers
like Michael Caine for instance

i may though think of the movie star John Wayne
"the hell i do"

i don't think of pop stars like Kurt Cobain
who's thinking of blowing out his brain

i don't think of drugs
and snorting cocaine

i don't think of Ireland
it's troubles, Sinn Fein

i don't think of the weather, the sun, the rain
or even something as strong as a hurricane

i don't think of riches
class or champagne

when i look up to the sky
and i see an aeroplane

i think of you
a stewardess from Finland
with the beauty of the Aurora Borealis
and it's magnetic light
in flight.

In these very sensitive times you are not allowed to take sharp objects onto an aeroplane. Because of this, they confiscate my razor at the security checkpoint. What were they expecting me to do, shave the pilot to death.

Next time I'll try a can opener.

The Rome Poems
or
Roems

My Girlfriend's Common Cold In Rome

she is snotty
and has a voice
like Pavarotti.

When In Rome

Fight lions
Bag a slave
Hail Caesar
Eat pomegranates
Glug on cheap wine at expensive prices
Participate in a gay orgy
Ride a chariot very fast around in a circle
Worship Gods
Become a month in the year – Danuary
Build straight roads
Civilise a chav
Pay the bill by cheque and write the amount in numerals
Try it on with an Egyptian Queen
Invade and conquer new worlds
But don't cross the border into Scotland
Just build a very long wall
Once past Newcastle the weather does deteriorate somewhat.
Get stabbed by some thugs
Set up a sewage system
Bathe in a steaming bath
Mosaic the floor
Put the central heating on
Order an army of one hundred men to cross the Alps on
    elephant
Have a go at pottery
Count on an abacus
Embrace fascism
Grease your hair back
Be macho yet a bit gay
Be proud of your appearance

Finishio allio ofio yourio wordios in 'i' or 'o'
Become a fashion designer
Drive a small car very badly
Finito.

Shopping

Newton's Law

an apple from a vending machine
must carry VAT
an apple from a tree – is free.

Retail Therapy

there should be a shop
where you can rent
a smile for a while
or a long weekend

there should be a place
where you can go
to buy a laugh
for a close friend

the receipts in the bag
so you can take it back
if it's the wrong one
or if it doesn't fit

is there an
out-of-town megastore
with giggles for sale
stacked high on shelves?

buy two chuckles
get one free

a scream of joy
with same day delivery

a laughter world
to upgrade your snigger
to make it much bigger

with 50% off
an ear-to-ear grin

titters for under a tenner
off the peg
or made to measure

a chortle on mail order

because sadness always seems to be
just around the corner.

Girls love handbags
though girls that wear combat trousers
tend to keep their belongings
in their pockets.

My girlfriend buys a handbag
every time she goes shopping.

We live in a small one bedroom flat.
We have no room for furniture
so we sit on handbags for comfort.

Art

Magritte Poem

this is not a poem

The Scream

after lunch
Eddie Munch
was casually sucking on a sweet
when 'CRUNCH!'
"oooh" Eddie screamed
and he dreamed to share this experience.
                                           hence

the sky blowing red
and Ed
whilst lying in bed
his tooth aching
and in the morning awaking
to pastel a picture
        a mixture
of curls
      twirls
            colour and swirls
a portrait of himself yelling
"oooh my tooth"
revealing the common belief
that you should look after your teeth
                            and gums.

but the world got the wrong end of the stick
on completion of this picture
believing it to be about Eddies sickening paranoia
                        and fears
      just from the way he's holding his ears

screaming
longing for a dentist
for where it was originally intended
for Eddie wanted his teeth mended.
so Ed
who was sensitive and gentle
                    mildly mental
            had extreme dental trouble
                    and no manly stubble
realised as he struggled on through the pain
that he was indeed
                    in need
of some help and companionship
to stop him from going insane.

so
he phoned his friend Vincent
Vincent Van Gogh
who cut his own ear off!
someone you could rely on to give sound advice.

and as Ed explained his predicament
and how nobody understood
Vincent who was gob smacked by what he heard
through his good ear
said "what you on about Ed
it's about your paranoia and fears
by the way you're holding your head and ears
let's go to the pub and talk over some."

so they talked
and Vincent chatted
and Ed accepted
that like Vincent
he too would never be fully understood
so he carried on drinking
and asked Vincent if he'd like another
"no thanks" Vincent replied
"I've got one ear!"

Defecated IKB 79
(Yves Klein Patent Blue)

i curled out a poo
on Yves Klein blue
i finished off with a fart
but is it art?

When Success Rears Its Ugly Head

A Vignette

I used to have malt vinegar
drizzled on the limp leaves of rabbit lettuce.
Now I have organic balsamic vinegar
and extra virgin olive oil sprinkled
on rocket leaves.

This is a vignette, not a vinaigrette.

Born To Perform

when I see a female
with large hooped ear-rings

I am transformed
into an acrobatic clown
performing in the big top
of a circus

I light a match
and set fire to her ear lobe
jump into the barrel
of a cannon
and ignite the fuse
'BOOM'

I fly through the air
somersaulting as I go
through the flaming hooped ear-ring
landing safely on the other side
with a forward roll
and to rapturous applause.

A Poem About Scott Walker

great singer
Scott Walker
not much of a talker

Jarvis Coffee

who did i meet
at Liverpool Street Station
one of the biggest pop stars
of our nation
Jarvis Cocker
drinking a Jarva Coffee

intrigued by his love of coffee
i ask, "hey Jarvis Cocker
do you like mochas?"

"yes" he replied, "but i don't like sarcasm."

Britney Spears

it will all end in Britney Spears
it will all end
in going down the pub for some Britneys
i had a nightmare
it revealed to me my worst Britney Spears

it's as clear as crystal
i can see through the mud
                  the dirt
              and grime
hit me baby one more time.

Rhyme Stone Cowboy

like a rhyme stone cowboy
i ride the plain
and from a distance
i look like John Wayne

"the hell i do!"

Familiarity breeds contempt.
I think it should be content.

Anecdotal Evidence

Class

the middle classes
are up their own arses

"I can't hear the TV.
What's he saying?
Can't hear it.
Wot-de' say?
Turn it up.
Turn it up.
Can't hear a thing.
I'm a bit deaf in one ear.
Can't hear.
Turn it up.
Where's the thingy?
You know the thingy-ma-jig?
Can't hear it.
Turn it up."

"Well if you stop talking and listen
you might hear what he's saying.
It's not coz you are deaf it's just
you keep on talking!"

"Oh be quiet, I can't hear the T.V."

TV Girl

she reads the news
she looks beautiful
when she mentions
a famine in Africa
or a dog stuck down
a local well.

she reads the weather
she looks vulnerable
when she mentions
a low front over Southern Wales
or heavy rain in Manchester.

Big Poem

Big Hitters   Big Stick
Big Bullies   Big Dick

Big Cock   Big Car
Big Shit   Big Star

Big Fish   Big Thoughts
Big Bucks   Big Noughts

Big Cheese   Big Deal
Big Shot   Big Kill

Big Apple   Big Smoke
Big Business   Big Joke

Big Wig   Big-ot
Big No No   Big Knot

Big Brother   Big Head
Big Bombs   Big Dead

Big Blunder   Big Slump
Big C   Big Lump

Big Boobs   Big Hips
Big Planes   Big Ships

Big Mouth   Big Mac
Big Woman   Big Crack

Big Bang   Big Top
Big Mistakes Big Stop

Stop
for a little thought
for little folk
a little laughter
a little joke

a little spittle
to help to stick
the broken
the brittle
the little
the sick.

Christmas At My Nan's

i never really understood
how the 20p got in the Christmas Pud
or how it always ended up in my Nan's slice
every time we spent Christmas round her house.

Evidence Of Santa

I saw straw
Scattered on the floor

Eye sore soot
Settled on the settee

Eye sore a hint
Of a muddy boot print
from winter snow

from what I can tell
I heard a single
jingle bell

Eye heard an aloof
hoof
on the roof

Now if that isn't proof!!!

Dooze And Don'ts

I don't do black
And I don't do white
I don't do flag
But I do do kite

I do do trust
Courage
Kindness
And love
I don't do religion
or heavens above
So I don't do Christian, Muslim or Jew
But what I do do
Is me and you
I dooby dooby do

I don't do test
I do do
do your best
I don't do string vest
Or stick out your chest

I do gay, straight, cross dressing, sex change
and girls as best mates
I don't do boundaries or shut gates
I do blind dates
I do single
Married
and living in sin

I do recycle
And I do "just throw it in the bin."

I don't do two for me and one for you
Or one for me and two for you
That I just don't do
I don't do unfair
I don't do nightmare
I don't do Tony Blair
I do do heart and care
And I do do
Cut, rip and tear

I don't do suit and tie
I do do tiny tiny, will anyone notice, little lie
Like 'my oh my you look fabulous in that dress'
And I do do cry

I do swim
I don't do running
And I don't do gym
It's boring

I do old
I do new
I do young
I do blue

I do above
I do below

I do shove
I do tow
I do just push it down the hill and let go
we'll see what happens!

I do foot
I do bike
I do bus, train, car, plane
any transport you like

I do scared
I do fear
I do laugh
I do tear

I do glad
I do sad
I do angry
I do I'm really really really really MAD!!!!

I do grumpy
I do lazy
I do busy
I do happy
I do really annoying
Childish
No I don't
Yes you do
No I don't
Yes you do
No I don't

Yes you do

I don't do jealousy
I do do crude
Rude
Insulting
And down right offensive
But usually not on purpose (you wankers)

I do early
I do late
I do fate
I do man love
you're my best mate
I love you

I do failure – really well
I do success
I do tidy
I do mess
I do more and I do less
More or less

I do the latest gossip
I do yesterdays news
I do win
I do lose
I do 'you choose'
And I do "oh can't we do something else"

I do generous
I do skint
I do "I can take a hint"
I don't do gold
I do do flint
I do English, Earl Grey and Peppermint

I do
I do do
And I do love you
And I don't want you to go.

it's not a landline
it's a phone

since when has it been a landline

it's a phone
not a landline.

The Aches Of An Alcoholic

Greenwich Park

he had writer
written all over him
wrapped in old paper
yesterdays discarded news
on a bench
in a park
after dark
a fifth of whiskey
a can of Stella
used to settle
and bring to a simmer
big brave thoughts
that boil over
to leave him standing
where he's sitting.

Memories

are
pickled
in a jar

snowflakes
in a room
melting on the floor

muddled up
      jigsaw puzzles
         with pieces missing
      and no picture
         on the front of the box
         for reference
some
are sparkling
crisp
clear
still
blue skied
horizons
you can place your thumb on it
but you can't touch it

some are newly sharpened pencils
as soon as you press
carbon
to paper
the lead snaps

some are rainbows
clouds
rivers
and roads

some are heavy loads

you carry them around
yet you can't put them down
like carrying an elephant
up a mountain

some are jokes
some hilarious
some like a comedy desert
not very funny

some are piggy banks
filled with lots of money

a safe deposit box
protected by a forgotten combination

an empty train station

a locked door
a down pour
a flash flood
a field full of mud

a famine

some are like standing at the bus stop
hoping and praying for a bus
please let there be a bus
please let there be a bus
to pass the time
you hum a tune
whistle a song
you wait all day
then three come along
                at once

some are a nagging mother
a constant reminder
you pretend not to care
but secretly
you are glad they are there

some you cradle in your arms
some you hold out in your palms

some you let slip from grasp like a helium balloon

some are hidden round the corner
and will happen very soon

Mobile Phone Poem

where are you?

everyone's alone
with their mobile phone
gone are the days
that you need to be connected
to a wall and socket
now it's off the hook
when you grab it from your pocket

where are you?

i'm on a rocket
heading towards Mars
i'll be home in ten minutes

the gardener is getting on the blower
where are you?
i'm mowing the lawn with my mower
can you hear me?
your voice is getting lower

i'm losing you
we're breaking up

alone
with my mobile dog and bone
a man's best friend
press end.

His blue room-to-grow-into-blazer swamped his boyish frame, his un-tucked shirt flapping at his knees. His hand-me-down trousers rose above the ankle, revealing dirty grey socks and scuffed black shoes, with enough space in them to rent a room or make any clown proud.

His appearance wasn't anything to be desired. Scruffy schoolboy.

Red Balloon

red balloon
float to the moon
i'm a loon
a loony tune
a lunar star
i'm way over par
i'm a D cup boob
in an A cup bra

Stability Poem

i'm as confident
as confetti
in it's box

i'm as happy
as a horologist
without any clocks

i'm lower
than a climber
with no rocks... to climb

i'm as wobbly
as a jelly
that's not set

i'm as open
as an office
that's to let

i'm as in love
as Romeo
who has not met Juliet

i've been found out
like the Bigfoot
has not Yet-i

i'm as bitter
as the time
i was chucked by Janette
who should visit a vet
coz i think she's a dog
and should be hit by a car
i'd rather an iguana
as a pet
and i hate them too
she's a degenerate.

i'm as refreshing
as a cup of tea
full of dregs

i'm as content
as a tent
with no pegs

i'm as complete
as a fry up
with no fried eggs

i'm as stable
as a table
with two legs.

The water in the tap isn't as clean as it should be. It has Mercury in it. I stick to lamp-posts when I walk past.

I think the bloke next door has killed his wife and kid. I haven't seen them for months, but I saw him once coming home drunk as if he couldn't handle what he was trying to hide.

Lazy

Job Hunt

In a desperate attempt to gain employment, I seriously consider taking up the position of Santa Claus in the grotto of the local shopping centre. Having been declined the job of Santa at the interview stage, I was then encouraged by the centres deputy manager to apply for the vacancy of Santa's Elf, as I was more appropriately suited in appearance to such a character. This comment dented my already very low self-esteem.

I skipped the fare on the Tuesday night nightbus. Confidently squeezed passed the driver in the sweep of the crowd. A minor victory, a meagre 70p saving that made me feel slightly better, helped ease the growing nausea, that I increasingly felt about the twenty thousand pound credit card debt I had hanging over me. But as my mother says, 'Every little helps!'

Writers Road Block

A13
A13
it's not where I'm going
it's just where I've been

A13
A13
it's a terrible scene
down the A13

unlucky for some
unlucky for me
I want to be heading
down the A23
south towards the sea

but instead I'm stuck
in traffic again
heading along
the A13

A13
A13
it's not where I'm going
it's just where I've been

A13
A13
it's a terrible scene
down the A13

if I can just make it
to the M25
I might just make it
out alive

and take me down
to the A23
BN1
by the sea

why didn't I
take the train
instead of struggling along
in the slow lane
of the A13

A13
A13
it's not where I'm going
it's just where I've been

A13
A13
it's a terrible scene
down the A13

Car Crash Victim Poem

I suck food through a straw
because I have a broken jaw.

she does Sudoku
on the loo
whilst searching for a number 2

The Other Ones

The Bath Bomb

my friend bought me a bath bomb
which would have been a laugh
but there is only one problem
that is I haven't got a bath
for my bath bomb
I can imagine the sensation
of the bubbles on my bum
this T.N.T. testicle tickler
it would of been oh so much fun
oh my beautiful bath bomb
what am I to do
use you in my shower of great power
or watch you ignite
as I flush you down the loo
BOOM BOOM to my bath bomb
how I dream of getting you into my warm tub
to observe closely your foaming bubbles
to take away my aches and all my troubles
bath bomb
you can heal me
relieve my pain
just like Jesus healed the blind
I would never smell again
oh great one
I worship my bath bomb

Poetry Is Good For You

don't just read poetry
or write poetry
eat poetry
let it satisfy your hunger

think poetry
drink poetry
suck it through a straw
pour it on the page
blow bubbles with it
until it comes out your nose

plant poetry
until it grows

recycle poetry
use it over and over again
lend it to a friend
steal it
reveal it
peel it
like a potato
learn the difference
between staccato and a cento
type it on a computer
or use a Biro

sleep poetry
dream poetry
sit on top of a poetry cloud

don't just leave poetry
under your bed
let it be said out loud

write good poetry
share it
write great poetry
publish it
write bad poetry
roll it into a ball
play poetry football with it

get good at football
play for England
write a poem about it
have 99% ball passion
instead of possession... much better.

jump on the poetry bus
crash a poetry car

fight poetry
wrestle poetry to the ground
throw it
flick it in the air
get it in your hair
lock it in a strangle hold
be bold
body slam it
until it submits

give poetry as a present
to someone you love
to someone who loves you
to someone you don't like very much
for example, a politician who is messing
things up for the rest of us.

remember
poetry is good for you
It will make you lots of friends
so eat it everyday
let it satisfy your hunger

spit it out if it tastes bad
consume it slowly
when it tastes good

don't just read it
or write it
place the world on your page
and light it
join words together
unite it.

Smiling Mouse Poem

MouseMouseMouseMouseMouseMouseMouseMouseMouseMouse
MouseMouseMouseMouseMouseMouseMouseMouseMouseMouse
MouseMouseMouseMouseMouseMouseMouseMouseMouseMouse
MouseMouseMouseMouseMouseMouseMouseMouseMouseMouse
MouseMouseMouseMouseMouseMouseMouseMouseMouseMouse
MouseMouseMouseMouseMouseMouseMouseMouseMouseMouse
MouseMouseMouseMouseMouseMouseMouseMouseMouseMouse
MouseMouseMouseMouseMouseMouseMouseMouseMouseMouse
MouseMouseMouseMouseMouseMouseMouseMouseMouseMouse
MouseMouseMouseMouseMouseMouseMouseMouseMouseMouse
MouseMouseMouseMouseMouseMouseMouseMouseMouseMouse
MouseMouseMouseMouseMouseMouseMouseMouseMouseMouse
MouseMouseMouseMouseMouseMouseMouseMouseMouseMouse
MouseMouseMouseMouseMouseMouseMouseMouseMouseMouse
MouseMouseMouseMouseMouseMouseMouseMouseMouseMouse
MouseMouseMouseMouseMouseMouseMouseMouseMouseMouse
MouseMouseMouseMouseMouseMouseMouseMouseMouseMouse
MouseMouseMouseMouseMouseMouseMouseMouseMouseMouse
MouseMouseMouseMouseMouseMouseMouseMouseMouseMouse
MouseMouseMouseMouseMouseMouseMouseMouseMouseMouse
MouseMouseMouseMouseMouseMouseMouseMouseMouseMouse
MouseMouseMouseMouseMouseMouseMouseMouseMouseMouse
MouseMouseMouseMouseMouseMouseMouseMouseMouseMouse
MouseMouseMouseMouseMouseMouseMouseMouseMouseMouse
MouseMouseMouseMouseMouseMouseMouseMouseMouseMouse
MouseMouseMouseMouseMouseMouseMouseMouseMouseMouse
MouseMouseMouseMouseMouseMouseMouseMouseMouseMouse
MouseMouseMouseMouseMouseMouseMouseMouseMouseMouse
MouseMouseMouseMouseMouseMouseMouseMouseMouseMouse
MouseMouseMouseMouseMouseMouseMouseMouseMouseMouse

Canvey Island

the ebb of tide
the rivers mouth
a sickness flows
flooding dykes with ignorance
waded through by locals
up to their necks in estuary

sick little island
Canvey Island-ed on it
oh lucky me

Sir Francis Drake floated past it
i missed it
he sailed on the Golden Hind
whilst mine was being tanned golden
by my dad

the people of Canvey are lost
they've got that sinking feeling
it's probably because they're thirty feet below
water level

with no wick left to graze on
it's safety in numbers
soon to be fish soup

a tall wall keeps out the water
preventing a flood
preventing Canvey from becoming the sea bed
instead it's just a shit hole

a tatty old mud flat
a shitty old marshland
Canvey Island-ed on it
oh lucky me.

Hampstead Heath Poem

i found a sheath
on Hampstead Heath
beneath
a leaf

A Worthy Epitaph

6/10
could of done better
see me.

After Thought

I think it's very weird
that my dad wears after-shave
even though he has a beard

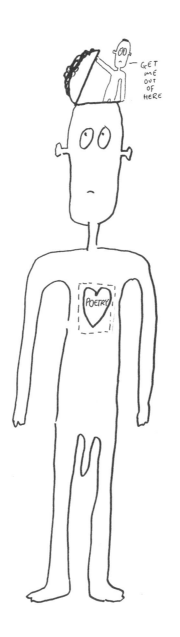